ASSERTIVENESS

Other titles in the Lifeskills Personal Development series:

Assertiveness – A Positive Process
Communication – Time to Talk
Preparing for Successful Learning
Relationships – A Question of Quality
Stress, Health and Your Lifestyle
Successful Learning in Action
Transitions – The Challenge of Change

ASSERTIVENESS

A Positive Process

Christine Beels,
Dr Barrie Hopson
and Mike Scally

MERCURY

can give it too. It's a positive way of behaving, that doesn't involve violating the rights of other people. Above all, assertive behaviour is *appropriate* behaviour. This can mean that it's appropriate on occasions to be angry, or it can mean choosing not to be assertive in a particular situation or with a particular person.

The way we act physically tells people a lot about us. Our body language often reveals how we feel and may show uncertainty, or contradict what we say. A good example is the person who says, 'I'm not angry', but the clenched teeth, rigid posture and grim expression reveal their feelings. Or what about the person who says, 'I really mean it', but refuses to look you in the eye? In cases like these, the body language contradicts the spoken words.

Can you think of another example?

....

....

Which do you think you are more likely to believe, the body language or the spoken words?

....

In fact, although we are not always conscious of body language, we instinctively respond to the body language rather than the words that are spoken.

Similarly, gestures such as fiddling with hair or biting nails, not looking at the other person, or hesitant, mumbling or indistinct speech can all undermine your efforts to assert yourself. How can we be sure that our body language does not contradict, or undermine, what we are trying to say?

The answer is to observe ourselves in everyday situations. When you find yourself using unhelpful body language, think how you could sit, stand and use your hands and facial expression to reinforce what you say. Practise speaking clearly and evenly: don't be ashamed of what you have to say — come right out and own it!

The following chart will help you to identify instances of body language which are positive or negative in each situation. You could mark each one with a + or −, depending on whether you think the effect will be good or bad.

	Posture	Facial Expression	Hands	Eyes	Tone of Voice
YOUNG PERSON: I've come about the job.	Slouching in chair or Standing upright	Smiling or Blank	Ready for handshake or Clasped together	Looking directly at person or Downcast eyes	Clear, firm or Mumbling
PARENT: I want you to tidy your room – now!	Turning away, busy or Facing child	Shaking head or Serious	Scratching head or Pointing	Glaring or Calm, straight look	Vague, unconcerned or Emphatic
EMPLOYEE: I'll finish this tomorrow – I've got to go now.	Facing boss or Rummaging in drawer	Calm or Laughing	Hands visible or Hands fiddling	Looking at fingers or Direct look	Quick, quiet speech or Direct, businesslike
SHOPPER: I've brought these goods back – they are faulty.	Head bowed, looking in bag or Head upright, facing assistant	Worried frown or Smiling	Showing goods or Stroking hair	Makes eye contact or Avoiding eye contact	Clearly spoken or Nervous, hesitant
IN A QUEUE: Excuse me, but I was next.	Standing square-on or Approaching from behind	Sad, despairing look or Smiling	Hands clenched, raised or Hands by side	Looking person in the eye or Looking at their shoes	Loud, accusing or Calm but clear

Thinking about the ways in which our behaviour can affect what we want to say helps us to 'unlearn' some unhelpful habits and adopt a more positive body language which will reinforce our spoken message. Did you notice that some examples came up again and again? That's because they are very effective ways of getting your message over clearly, politely and without causing offence: smiling, for example.

Checklist of Helpful Body Language

- **Facial Expression:** while smiling helps enormously to reinforce that what you say is meant constructively, you should always be genuine – do not smile if you are sad, angry or serious.

- **Eyes and gaze:** the ability to look someone directly in the face and maintain eye contact shows openness and sincerity; looking away will almost always undermine your message.

- **Posture:** Standing square-on, facing the other person, with head held high is direct and open; turning away, slouching or an unbalanced stance show lack of interest or commitment.

- **Hand and arm movements:** avoid fiddling as this distracts attention from your message and from your sincerity; use hands to emphasise what you say in a helpful (but not an aggressive) way.

- **Tone of voice:** whispering, rushing or mumbling all suggest that you doubt what you are saying; speak up clearly and confidently in an even tone of voice.

- **Own what you say:** 'Owning' what you say means making it clear that this is your own opinion, not someone else's, and not what you think someone might like to hear. For example, compare these two conversations between boyfriend and girlfriend:

A.   'Where would you like to go tonight?'
     'Wherever you like – they say that new Italian restaurant is quite good.'

B.   'Where would you like to go tonight?'
     'I'd really like to go to that new restaurant.'

In example A, the questioner is no wiser about what the other person feels and has no opportunity to please that person. In example B, the questioner gets a clear answer, knows what the other person would like and can agree or disagree. Clear statements which begin 'I think' or 'I would like' are more helpful to the other person.

In some situations, it might be that co-operative words and phrases are more suitable. By co-operative phrases, we mean words that might encourage someone to work or act with you rather than against you. Think of a situation where you want someone to co-operate with you. What kind of co-operative phrases could you use rather than, 'you do this and I'll do that'?

....

....

....

You might have suggested:

'We could . . .'
'Shall we . . .?'
'Let's try to . . .'

A few more words on appropriateness:

Assertive behaviour is behaviour that is suitable, or appropriate, for the occasion. It involves being able to express what we want without feeling unduly anxious or hesitant. This is not the same as being 'totally honest' about our feelings. Neither is it lying. It is a nice balance – being able to express what you feel without offending others or contravening the norms of the situation.

Appropriateness is a social skill that matters a lot, particularly when learning to be an assertive person. Assertiveness is not a licence for bursts of uncontrollable anger because things are not as you think they should be. If there are many 'shoulds' and 'oughts' in your life, either about yourself or about other people, then you would probably benefit from looking at why you hem yourself in with 'I should be . . .' or 'I ought to . . .' You do have the right to be annoyed if someone has violated your rights, but the skill lies in expressing this constructively and, as we are saying, appropriately.

What is Aggressive Behaviour?

What words come to mind when you look at this question?
Write all the words you can think of to describe aggressive behaviour in this box:

Do your words for aggressive behaviour refer to body language, tone of voice or other attempts to dominate the situation? Do you like aggressive behaviour? No – and we certainly don't like being on the receiving end, whether it's words or actions that are used. Assertive behaviour is *not* aggressive behaviour.

Aggressive behaviour is the kind that expresses feelings and opinions in a way which punishes, threatens or puts the other person down. The aim of this behaviour is for the person to get their own way, no matter what. When we are sarcastic, manipulative, when we spread gossip or make racist or sexist remarks, we are behaving as aggressively as when we bully or push. If we win, and get what we want, it probably leaves someone else with the bad feeling that they have lost. Aside from any ethical considerations, this could auger badly for us in future trans-actions with that person. Another possible consequence of behaving aggressively is that we might feel guilty later.

Aggressive people often stand too close to others, or they stand when others sit, they point or wag their fingers and use a loud, hectoring tone of voice. They may pat people (on the shoulder for instance) which is patronising and reduces the other person's status.

Politicians often demonstrate aggressive behaviour very well!

Using your personal experience, can you note two examples of aggressive ways of beginning a conversation? Write your answers in the following space.

....

....

....

We thought of:

> 'You must . . .'
> 'You should . . .'
> 'You ought . . .'
> 'You've got to . . .'
> 'Why haven't you . . .?'

You'll see that, unlike the assertive person, the aggressive person doesn't 'own' what he or she says. Rather, an aggressive person immediately transfers the blame to someone else, or directly orders others about without regard for their feelings.

Why are we Aggressive?

We can all become aggressive when we feel threatened or in the wrong. Aggression is usually a sign that there is something wrong with the aggressor, whether they simply got out of bed on the wrong side, or something has gone badly wrong with their lives. If you find yourself resorting to aggressive behaviour, ask yourself what is wrong and why you are projecting your bad feelings on to someone else. Take time out to think of more constructive ways of handling whatever has gone wrong.

What is Unassertive Behaviour?

In what ways are we sometimes unassertive? How do we show it? Think hard, and write down some of the times you have felt unassertive, and the ways you showed it, in the space below:

We have noted some pluses and minuses of behaving assertively, and of appropriate behaviour, briefly looked at why we are not all naturally assertive, and what the consequences of unassertive behaviour can be.

Can you jot down here two things you have thought or learned about yourself as a result of working through the book so far?

1. ....

2. ....

Section Two: Ways of Getting What I Want

In the last Section, we identified the three main routes people use to get what they want or need. In this section, we are inviting you to complete a short quiz. Each situation has three possible answers; we're asking you to decide whether each response is an example of assertive, aggressive or unassertive behaviour. Jot down what category of behaviour you think each response belongs to – we will provide the answers afterwards!

1   You are wearing your new dress/suit. You like it a great deal and are pleased when your friend says that she thinks it is terrific. You say:

a)   Thanks. I'm glad you like it, because I really do.
b)   Oh this! It's nothing special.
c)   Oh! I . . . got it cheap in a sale . . .

2   Your secretary has begun to produce letters badly set out with many errors. You say:

a)   Your work's been appalling this week. Whatever's the matter with you?
b)   I've been surprised by your work this week. There have been a lot of typing errors. Can we talk about it?
c)   These letters are really not good enough. You're getting careless – or lazy.

3   A colleague asks to borrow your car. You would rather not lend out your car. You say:

a)   Well . . . OK . . . I suppose it's alright.
b)   You've got a cheek. Of course you can't. Get your own car.
c)   I'd rather not. I'm a bit possessive about it. I might be being silly, but I'd still rather not. I'm sorry.

4   You would like your friend to pick up a newspaper for you on his way to your house. You say:

a)   Would you mind picking up an evening paper on your way over here? I'd really appreciate that.
b)   I don't suppose you're passing a . . . oh never mind, it's not important.
c)   I really want a paper, but I don't have time to get it myself.

5   You have met a person you like very much and want to go out with her. You meet her. You say:

a)   I'd really like to go out with you. How about Saturday?
b)   Well, what are you doing with yourself these days?
c)   I hear there's a good film at the Odeon this week.

6   You are taking a damaged record back to the store. The salesperson says it must be your fault. You know that it was faulty when you first played it. You say:

a)   It sounded like this the first time I played it. I don't see how it can be my fault. I would like a new copy.
b)   Don't be ridiculous. I wouldn't try to put one over on you. Are you calling me a liar?
c)   Oh, alright.

7   Equipment is in very short supply in your department. You have bought some pens yourself and put them down in the office. A junior colleague comes in, picks them up and walks off . . . You say:

a)   Excuse me . . . oh . . . (under your breath) well, she's young . . . not her fault . . .
b)   I'm sorry, but actually those pens are mine. I really shouldn't have put them down there.
c)   Hi, those pens are mine. Can I have them back please?

Answers:

I   a) Assertive. You are pleased that someone likes it and you accept the compliment.
     b) Unassertive. You are embarrassed at the compliment and try to negate it.
     c) Unassertive. You are embarrassed at the compliment and try to negate it.

2   a) Aggressive. You launch an attack with no consideration of a previously high standard.
     b) Assertive. You acknowledge previous good work, state your disssatisfaction clearly and invite comment.
     c) Aggressive. You make unhelpful critical comments.

3   a) Unassertive. You will most likely feel bad later, or angry at your colleague for asking you. He is being assertive. You are not.

     b) Aggressive. You can refuse without putting him down.

     c) Assertive. He might not like it, but that is the way you are. He knows where he stands and also that in the future you can be relied upon to be honest and straight.

4   a) Assertive. He always has the right to refuse.

     b) Unassertive. Assume that he will refuse if it is inconvenient. If he will not, then it is about time he learned to be assertive!

     c) Unassertive. You are trying to manipulate him into offering. He may not be aware of your intentions or may be annoyed that you are being devious.

5   a) Assertive.

     b) Unassertive. You are backing off from asking for what you really want. The likelihood is, therefore, that you will not get it.

     c) Unassertive. Your message is not clear. She is having to guess what you really want. If she wants it too, it puts her in a difficult situation. She might worry that she is wrong and so may not be assertive enough to take the risk of following it up. You are basically trying to manipulate her to ask you!

6   a) Assertive. You are standing up for your rights. You know you are not to blame and you have the right as a consumer to get satisfaction. You are not getting angry with the salesperson, because it is not her fault.

     b) Aggressive. You will either frighten or annoy the salesperson. If you frighten her you are walking over her; if you anger her you are less likely to get her co-operation.

     c) Unassertive. You are being walked upon.

7   a) Unassertive. Don't you want your pens?

     b) Unassertive. There's no need to apologise. Your apologetic manner may make your colleague embarrassed.

     c) Assertive. A quick, straightforward (smiling) response defuses a potentially awkward situation.

How did you do in gauging the different responses? Make a note in the space below of any learning points that you picked up as a result of this activity.

Checklist: Assertive, Aggressive and Unassertive Behaviour

ASSERTIVE	AGGRESSIVE	UNASSERTIVE
You Do:	**You Do:**	**You Do:**
• ask for what you want,	• try to get what you want,	• hope that you will get what you want,
• directly and openly,	• in any way that works,	• sit on your feelings,
• appropriately,	• often give rise to bad feelings in others,	• rely on others to guess what you want.
• have rights,		
• ask confidently and without undue anxiety.	• threaten, cajole, manipulate, use sarcasm, fight.	**You Don't:**
You Don't:	**You Don't:**	• ask for what you want,
• violate other people's rights,	• respect that other people have a right to get their needs met,	• express your feelings,
• expect other people to guess what you want,		• usually get what you want,
• freeze up with anxiety.	• look for situations in which you both might be able to get what you want ('win-win situations').	• upset anyone,
		• get noticed.

Describe below any recent situation in which your response was not assertive.

The situation: ....

....

I said: ....

....

What I would prefer to have said: ....

....

Personal Project

It is important at this stage in the workbook to begin to practise what you are reading about. Over the next few days look out for situations where you are asked to do something which you don't want to do, but which you would normally agree to. When this happens, instead of saying 'yes', say 'no', using the assertive manner that was described in our quiz. (You might have noticed that assertive refusals don't usually contain the word 'no'!) Return to this page when you have completed the project, and fill in the spaces below.

I felt: ....

....

....

S/he said: ....

....

....

In the end: ....

....

....

Summary

The quiz gave you different responses for a range of situations from the classic scenario of returning faulty goods through to asking a small favour. We hope you remember (from Section One) that how you stand, your tone of voice, and the expression on your face all contribute to the overall impression you make. For example, in the last question the assertive response could sound aggressive if a sharp unsmiling tone was used. We invited you to begin to practise more assertive behaviour.

Section Three: You Have Rights

We talked in the last section about rights and responsibilities. You cannot change your behaviour without also having an effect on others – an effect they may not like, or that might take some getting used to. Therefore it's important to be aware of both your rights and your responsibilities to others.

All human beings have rights. We're entitled to them by virtue of our very existence. In 1948, the United Nations proclaimed 30 Articles as a Universal Declaration of Human Rights. They cover broad and very basic issues: the right to life, liberty, a home, education, health, etc. Only a few of them have been achieved worldwide, but they exist as a benchmark for humankind.

Experts on psychology and how the human mind grows and develops would say that in our relationships with other people we are bound to have expectations of them. Just as a child expects the parent to look after it, so we have expectations in our relationships. We expect our friends to behave considerately. We have a right to such reasonable expectations. We do not have a right to unreasonable expectations such as a person giving up a cherished pastime for us! What is reasonable and unreasonable is a matter of judgment for each of us, but, by allowing others the same rights as we expect for ourselves, we can be fairly sure that our expectations of each other will be reasonable.

The Rights which we list on the next page may seem quite ordinary and acceptable when you first read them, but it can take a long time for some of these rights to sink in, and for you to accept them for yourself, as well as for other people. Look at the list and sign it: these are your rights and you are entitled to them. It helps to read them through often, for example, at times when you feel assailed by doubts over the rights and wrongs of your assertive behaviour.

Try reading the list aloud to yourself.

I Have the Right . . .

1   I have the right to ask for what I want (recognising that other people have the right to say No).

2   I have the right to have my own opinions and values and to express them appropriately.

3   I have the right to change my mind.

4   I have the right to make my own decisions and to cope with the consequences.

5   I have the right to decline responsibility for other people's problems.

6   I have the right to be successful.

7   I have the right to privacy, to be alone and to be independent.

8   I have the right to say 'I don't know' and 'I don't understand'.

9   I have the right to change myself and to be an assertive person.

10   I have the right to say 'No' and to say 'Yes' without feeling guilty.

11   I have the right to relate to others without being dependent on them for approval.

Signed ....

Date ....

Did you read the list aloud? Did you sign the declaration? What do you feel about these eleven statements?

....

....

....

Many people have little difficulty in accepting these rights for others, but the way they lead their lives shows that they do not accept them for themselves.

We can be overly tolerant and quick to make excuses:

- 'Well, he'll know better next time . . .'
- 'You're only young once . . .'
- 'She probably didn't realise . . .'

but we don't always make those same excuses about ourselves!

- 'I'm 40 years old. You'd think I'd have learned by now . . .'
- 'I should have kept my big mouth shut . . .'
- 'I'm so stupid. I never get anything right the first time . . .'

Can you look again at 'I Have the Right' and note here whether you feel comfortable with each one, or whether there are ways in which you don't accord yourself the degree of respect to which you are entitled. Perhaps you have examples to jot down?

My Thoughts:

1 ....

2 ....

3 ....

4 ....

5 ....

6 ....

7 ....

8 ....

9 ....

10 ....

11 ....

What have you written down? Are you happy that the list of Rights reflects the way you feel about yourself? Or are you worried and secretly afraid that, for instance, you don't have the right to privacy, or the right to say 'No'? It can certainly seem that way at times – when you're caring for young children, for example, it is well-nigh impossible to get any privacy or time to yourself. Using this as an example, think of two ways you could make time for some privacy without abandoning the family, friends or colleagues and their needs:

....

....

....

....

A Few Words on Responsibility

This example shows clearly that each of these personal rights has its concomitant responsibility. Firstly, you have the responsibility for the welfare of the children, family or colleagues, to see that their needs are met. Secondly, you have a responsibility to yourself – to make the decision and the arrangements for your privacy. We only achieve our rights when we shoulder the accompanying responsibility – and when we do, we become stronger, more capable of being proactive and more in control of our own lives.

What other responsibilities can you see arising from this list of rights?

....

....

....

....

....

The list of Rights becomes less daunting when you realise that it works both ways: if you can say 'No' to others, they also will expect the right to say 'No' to you. Having the right, in effect, gives you the responsibility of choice. For example, the right to decline responsibility for other people's problems may seem uncaring until you recognise that having the right is not the same as *always* declining responsibility for other people's problems. But for those of us who give in again and again to the sometimes selfish demands of others, this right gives us the choice of declining without feeling guilty. We are then in a position to make responsible choices instead of being manipulated by others.

Rather than giving a list of responsibilities that go along with these rights, perhaps we can simply say:

I have a responsibility to accord these rights to myself and others.

Summary

This section has outlined the rights and responsibilities of the assertive person. While it may be difficult at first to accept you have these rights, not giving yourself these rights can lead to passive behaviour. Not expecting others to accord you these rights can allow them to behave aggressively towards you.

You may need to return to this section and read it again, or to remind yourself of your rights from time to time, before you can begin fully to accept your own ability to allow yourself and other people these rights.

Section Four: Being Assertive

You have already learned a lot about assertiveness, but have you started to put it into practice yet? Let's take a measure of where you are now. The following questionnaires will help you to measure how assertive you are in your work and in your home life. You can fill out one or both questionnaires – using both will enable you to make comparisons such as 'am I more assertive at home or at work?'

How Assertive am I at Work?

AT WORK I FIND IT EASIER WITH:	PEOPLE 'SENIOR' TO ME	PEOPLE 'JUNIOR' TO ME	OTHER COLLEAGUES	YOUNGER PEOPLE	ADMIN/ ANCILLARY STAFF	OTHERS
TO EXPRESS POSITIVE FEELINGS BY: • telling them that I appreciate them						
• giving praise/compliments						
• receiving praise openly and without embarrassment						
• making requests						
• starting conversations						
TO EXPRESS NEGATIVE FEELINGS BY: • showing annoyance						
• showing I feel hurt						
TO STAND UP FOR MY RIGHTS BY: • refusing requests						
• refusing to be 'put down'						
• offering my opinion						
• making complaints						

√ FOR USUALLY   × FOR SELDOM

Who do you find it easiest to be assertive with?

....

Why do you think this is?

....

....

....

Who is it hardest to be assertive with?

Why do you think this is?

....

....

....

How Assertive am I at Home?

AT HOME I FIND IT EASIER WITH:	PARTNER	FRIENDS	PARENTS/ CHILDREN	OTHER RELATIVES	PEOPLE IN AUTHORITY	PEOPLE WHO PROVIDE SERVICES
TO EXPRESS POSITIVE FEELINGS BY: • telling them that I appreciate them						
• giving praise/compliments						
• receiving praise openly and without embarrassment						
• making requests						
• starting conversations						
TO EXPRESS NEGATIVE FEELINGS BY: • showing annoyance						
• showing I feel hurt						
TO STAND UP FOR MY RIGHTS BY: • refusing requests						
• refusing to be 'put down'						
• offering my opinion						
• making complaints						

√ FOR USUALLY   × FOR SELDOM

Women may have difficulty:

- expressing anger
- with being assertive (rather than manipulative)
- with authority figures and with being one.

Men may have difficulty:

- talking about vulnerability or weakness
- about errors they've made
- with women who are in a position of authority over them.

Appropriate Assertiveness

Now, let's move on to look at the questionnaire in the light of *appropriate behaviour*. Can you recall two of the points we made about appropriateness in Section One?

1 ....

2 ....

If you consider the people and the behaviours on your questionnaire, you will probably realise that with some people and in some situations, assertive behaviour won't work.

Looking back at the answers to your questionnaires, think of three types of situations where assertiveness may not work, or three kinds of people it does not work with:

....

....

....

Do these three examples have anything in common?

....

How can you deal with these situations?

....

In these situations we still have choices, depending upon who the people are and how they are behaving. If they are behaving aggressively, we can either resort to 'tit for tat', or we can continue to behave assertively (and fairly) in the hope they will learn from our example. The latter would provide a better role model for children – but what about the person in authority? In this case, remember your rights, particularly your right to decline responsibility for another's problems. Make an assertive choice not to get involved in a confrontation; you have the right to steer your own course.

Being assertive may not always be the most effective way of getting what you want with some people – especially people who are not assertive themselves.

Consider again the behaviours from the questionnaires on pages 30 and 31. Can you tick those which seem to you to be the most socially acceptable?

		√ here
1.	Express appreciation	☐
2.	Give praise/compliments	☐
3.	Receive praise with pleasure	☐
4.	Make requests	☐
5.	Initiate conversations	☐
6.	Show annoyance	☐
7.	Show hurt feelings	☐
8.	Refuse requests	☐
9.	Refuse to be put down	☐
10.	Offer opinions	☐
11.	Make complaints	☐

We suggest ticks beside numbers 1 to 5. Numbers 6 and 7, while they may be valid expressions of feeling on occasion, are not so socially acceptable, and numbers 8 to 11 are about our rights, which may sometimes conflict with the perceived or expressed needs of other people. This is why appropriateness is so important.

From this list, it is clear that being assertive about negative feelings and standing up for our rights tend to be less socially acceptable than the expressing of positive feelings.

We have to be very careful before we launch ourselves on everyone of our acquaintance, displaying our new assertiveness! It could be counter-productive.

Increase Assertiveness by Expressing More Positive Feelings First.

People will be more prepared to listen to negative feelings, or to our requests for our rights, after they have heard positive things from us about themselves. Can you select someone from the questionnaire to whom you want or may need to say something negative? What can you say first that's positive to him/her?

....

....

Is there anyone else, in either the 'Negative' section or the 'Rights' section, to whom you can also find something positive to say?

....

If your Manager needed to say something negative or critical to you, what positive thing would you like him or her to say first? Something good about your work?

I'd like to hear: ....

....

Summary

From this questionnaire you will have discovered or clarified more about yourself as an assertive person, and noted areas to work on. We briefly looked at assertive behaviour in the workplace and acknowledged the differences race and gender make.

We looked at appropriateness as a vital social skill and adjunct to assertive behaviour. We noted that:

- some people will not like assertive behaviour, because it is not in their interests
- we need to behave appropriately with different people, for example with parents or an employer
- we can begin to be more assertive by expressing our positive feelings about people first. They may then be more receptive to negative feelings.

Can you jot down here the two *main* learning points for you from this section.

....

....

Section Five: How Can I Start to be More Assertive?

The Skills So Far

This section summarises the skills we have already examined, and asks you to plan when and how you will put them into practice. This advance planning will make it easier for you when you try out what you have learned.

1. **Know What You Want To Say:** You won't appear confident if you are unsure of what you want. You could appear foolish by asking for something that you eventually realise is not what you want.

2. **Say It:** Don't hesitate or beat about the bush, come right out with it! Practise before you say it and check for appropriateness.

3. **Be Specific:** Say exactly what you want or do not want, so that there can be no confusion. Begin with the word 'I'. No long explanations are necessary.

4. **Say It as Soon as Possible:** Do not let too much time pass, as this builds up apprehension. On the other hand, do not say it at the peak of your anger. Wait for that to pass.

5. **Look The Person in the Eye:** People feel more comfortable if you look directly at them. You simply look shifty if you cannot look them in the eye. You certainly will not come across as someone who knows what they want.

6. **Look Relaxed:** You'll convey anxiety by shifting from one foot to another, waving your arms around, or conversely being too rigid. Practise looking relaxed in a mirror – it's not as contradictory as it sounds!

7. **Avoid Laughing Nervously:** Smile if it's appropriate, but if you giggle or laugh you won't look as if you mean what you say. This will confuse the person you are speaking to.

8. **Don't Whine or be Sarcastic:** Be direct and honest. Whining and pleading can either annoy the person or make them feel guilty. It is being manipulative. Being sarcastic, on the other hand, communicates hostility as you put the other person down.

> Note here the skills which you feel reasonably confident about, and think you can use:

Now, you have to practise all these dimensions of assertive behaviour – and put together all the different components of *the positive process*. We suggest that you look again at the questionnaire you completed in Section Three. Is there a 'people' column and a 'situations' column with quite a number of Xs in it? We would like you now to complete the following, using people and situations from the questionnaire. Take your time and visualise the scenario as you complete the spaces below.

The situation is: ....

....

1. Know what you want to say

What I want to say to: ....

is: ....

....

2. Say it!

The sentence I will use is: ....

....

....

3. Be specific

Check your first sentence; if it is not crystal clear, you might have to repeat the statement more clearly, being more specific. How might you re-word it, starting with the word 'I'? Concentrate on exactly what you want out of the situation.

....

....

....

4. Say it as soon as possible

Choose your time and place appropriately: it may not be helpful to grab someone in the corridor at work, or when someone is tired or busy. Choose a setting which will help you feel at ease and able to use the body language we have discussed – but don't put if off!

I will speak to: ....

on: ....

5. Look the person in the eye

6. Look relaxed

7. No nervous laughing

Imagine the setting you have chosen and how you will be sitting or standing. Imagine you are facing them. Practise your sentence (nos. 2 and 3 above) out loud. Look at yourself in the mirror – don't laugh! How does it feel? What will you do if the person takes no notice?

8. Don't whine or be sarcastic

If your response tends towards this, make a note here of how you can change this, bearing in mind the information on body language and tone of voice you already have.

....

....

....

Summary

In this Section, we have expanded on what you actually need to do to be more assertive, listing the skills and giving you an opportunity to visualise putting them into practice.

Having visualised the scene will put you more in command of yourself. But of course you cannot control the other person and must accept that some people cannot handle your assertiveness.

If this happens, don't be disappointed; there are several ways of handling it. First, if this is the kind of person with whom assertiveness makes no difference, then try an easier situation for yourself. Visualise it again – and then try it. Practice in the easier situations will build your confidence for dealing with people who cannot cope with assertive behaviour. Introduce yourself (and them) gently to your new assertive skills.

Finally, the next section will show you some additional skills for dealing with really intransigent situations. Read on!

Section Six: Skill Sharpening

In this Section we tell you more of the fundamental skills of assertive behaviour and suggest ways in which you can practise them. Changing behaviour isn't easy and, if we are moving from being an unassertive person to one who is more aware of our needs and rights, people who just want a handy doormat will initially be resistant to any changes in us!

Broken Record

We will look first at the skill of being persistent (sometimes called *Broken Record*). This is the skill of repeating over and over what you want or need, until you achieve it, or can negotiate. Being persistent won't lead to great intellectual debate, in fact it can be really irritating to the other people involved, but it's very useful when your *time* and your *energy* are valuable to you (which is most of the time!).

For example:

- when you want to get children to bed
- when you don't want to work late to help out a colleague
- when you have faulty goods to return to a shop.

Can you now take one straightforward incident in your own daily life (simple ones are best to start with) where you'd like to be persistent. Write it down here:

....

....

Now devise one or two clear straightforward sentences that will help you respond to the situation. Write them here:

....

....

....

....

Rehearse these sentences. Say them several times. Look at yourself in a mirror, remembering what you learned in Section One about body language.

When you have practised a sentence, slightly altering the words so that it doesn't sound too contrived, practise using it together with a sentence which *empathises* with the other person

41

(this shows that you're aware that they've got a problem, even though you are not going to resolve it for them).

You could try to role-play the situation with a friend. Explain the situation to them so that they can take the part of the other person; they can keep coming back at you, trying to get you to change your mind. You can keep repeating the same basic point back at them, in slightly different ways, until they get the message. The following example will give you the idea. While you're reading it, look out for the ways that Martin tries to wheedle and put pressure on Roger. Note how Roger handles this by repeating the same message in different ways – and how he shows some empathy for Martin's problem while refusing to take it on board himself.

Martin: 'I've got to get away early and the chief's just given me this report. You'll finish it
(4.30pm)   off for me won't you? It shouldn't take you too long.'

Roger: 'That's difficult for you, but I want to get away on time myself today.'

Martin: 'But I've absolutely got to meet someone – well, that girl, Natalie. Are you doing anything else tonight?'

Roger: 'I really want to get away on time myself tonight.'

Martin: 'Well, I don't know Rog, you always seem to be hanging around – I thought you liked to help out.'

Roger: 'Yes, I do like to help out, but tonight I want to get away on time.'

Three minutes later, Martin goes away to ask someone else.

Are there any points about this 'conversation' that you can jot down here?

....

....

....

You might have noted:

- that it's tedious to be on the receiving end of someone using Broken Record!

- that Roger didn't let himself be side-tracked at all; he didn't say whether he was, or wasn't, doing anything else that evening. It wasn't relevant to the fact that he didn't want to work late. *Keep to the point.*

- Roger acknowledged the truth of Martin's slight 'dig' about helping out, but immediately returned to the Broken Record.

● how little energy Roger used compared with either arguing with Martin or 'giving in' and feeling downtrodden (which uses tremendous amounts of energy).

The Broken Record can be useful in a meeting – the kind where red herrings are constantly strewn across the path. Subtle persistence can bring the attention of the meeting back to the subject you want.

Managing the Put-down

The second skill we introduce you to in this section is how to manage the put-down (or, if you prefer a more technical heading, stopping manipulative criticism and protecting your self-esteem).

Did you notice the attempt at a put-down or a diversionary side-swipe in the conversation used in the previous pages? Martin said to Roger that he always seemed to be hanging around – 'I thought you liked to help out'. Roger could have replied indignantly 'I don't hang around, what are you talking about – I'm just very hard-working – unlike some people!' If he had said that, the conversation would have taken a very different turn and Roger would undoubtedly have come out of it rather the worse for wear!

Recognising the put-down

Sometimes, people are trying to boost their own poor self-esteem by knocking ours, sometimes the put-down is well disguised as a joke, or as a traditional comment. At other times it is more blatant. Does all this seem a little like a War Zone? You may think that people don't really behave like this, but look at the following list of put-downs. Do they sound familiar?

'You're just like your mother'
'When you're my age . . .'
'I know I can rely on you . . .'
'Typical woman'
'Come on, it's only a bit of fun . . .'
'You look beautiful when you're angry . . .'
'You (whatever) are all the same . . .'

The trouble with put-downs is you don't always recognise them immediately, but after the conversation is over you might think to yourself 'What did they mean by that?' This after-effect needlessly reawakens your private fears and doubts about yourself.

Sometimes a put-down is disguised as a compliment: 'Michael's got a great sense of humour – it's a laugh a minute with him' or, 'How nice to be young and irresponsible'. It's a no-win situation: if you do ask the speaker what they mean by their remark, you may well be fobbed off with 'It was only a joke. Why do you take everything so personally?' This is, in effect, a double put-down because it now suggests that not only are you stupid and irresponsible but you are over-sensitive as well!

Can you add a couple of phrases that you have said to someone, or maybe had said to you, which would fall into this category?

....

....

....

....

Dealing with the put-down

The temptation for us all is to think of brilliant, cutting remarks that we could have made in reply. But after the event is too late and we are just wasting our mental energy on self-recrimination, such as, 'Why didn't I think of saying that at the time?' Even if you could think up a suitable put-down yourself at the time, this is simply falling into the trap of aggressive behaviour and is ultimately counter-productive for both you and them.

If this is happening to you and you cannot manage an assertive reply at the time, do not worry! When you have had time to think it over, you can take the person aside and tell them assertively how you feel about their remark. Remembering your list of Rights will help you, as will the techniques of 'negative enquiry' and 'fogging' which follow next.

Here is a short list of familiar put-downs; there is a hidden message and an assertive response to each.

The Put-down	The Hidden Message	You Say
If I were you . . .	I'm smarter than you!	But you're not me!
If only you'd *co-operate* . . .	*You* have to fall into *line with me.*	How can *we* co-operate?
You're not going to like this . . .	I'm going to make you tense/angry before I start . . .	I'll choose my own response.
That will be difficult for you won't it, because you can be a bit bossy . . .	I have the right to give you criticism you didn't ask for.	In what ways do you think I'm bossy?

Negative Enquiry

You probably noticed that in number 4 of the put-downs the response was in the form of a question. This is called *Negative Enquiry*. You actively seek criticism of your behaviour – but only if you're prepared for a straight answer. (Sometimes it's helpful to ask for criticism but that's another whole book in itself!) If your critic wasn't sincere, then your question will be fobbed off: 'Oh, I didn't mean it' or 'Oh, just my little joke'.

Are you getting the idea? Can you give an answer to these situations?

The Put-down	The Hidden Message	You Say
Are you busy tonight?	Got you! Your time's not valuable like mine . . .	
I know I'm being nosey, but . . .	I've got more rights than you, you're weak . . .	

We hope you have suggested something like: 'What did you have in mind?' This is a bit like Negative Enquiry; it is not seeking criticism, but it definitely calls their bluff!

For the second one, we hope you have suggested something like: 'Well, I won't tell you if I don't want to.' The other person hides their put-down of you by pretending to put themselves down! Don't be drawn into this game; make your position clear. You have the right to choose whether to tell them or not, once you know what they are trying to find out.

Fogging

This is a useful technique to use when the put-down has some truth in it, but has been exaggerated. For example:

'Your desk is in a real mess. It looks chaotic when clients call. It gives a really bad impression of the whole department. It's typical of your attitude!'

If there is truth in the accusation, your assertive response is to accept the grain of truth – but not the put-down. You could say:

'Yes. My desk is untidy. I'll clear it today.'

You don't need to rise to the bait about your attitude with protestations about how hard you work, though you could say:

'Yes. My desk is untidy – I've been busy. I'll clear it today.'

Can you note here three criticisms that people make of you, or that you are constantly afraid may be made of you. What response, using Fogging or Negative Enquiry, could be made to each of them?

Criticism	Response
1	1
2	2
3	3

Summary

In this Section, we have looked at skill sharpening techniques. Firstly, we looked at the important skill of persistence (Broken Record), to use when time and energy are valuable, or we don't want to become over-involved in a situation. We then went on to look at a number of general examples of how to recognise and handle manipulative criticism and attacks to self-esteem. We then had a brief look at Negative Enquiry and Fogging as counters to a put-down.

Can you note here two learning points for you from this Section?

1 ....

2 ....

What action can you take on what you've just written?

1 ....

2 ....

When will you take this action?

....

Section Seven: Criticism and Compliments

Most of us find it very difficult to take criticism, and it can be just as hard when you have to dish it out. Often this stems from our childhood experience of criticism, which may have been accompanied by feelings of blame, guilt and fear of rejection. Even as adults, we still experience criticism as withdrawal of approval, affection and esteem. It hurts!

The first way to take the sting out of criticism is to distinguish between valid and invalid criticism.

Valid Criticism

Valid criticism is criticism that you know to be fair, because you really did arrive late or forget your papers, or you weren't listening, or you really have been irritable or snappy lately. In this case, learn to accept that the criticism is valid and that it only criticises one aspect of your behaviour and does not reject you as a person.

Help yourself to accept the truth of the criticism by agreeing openly with it. You do not have to run and hide, seek excuses or apologise for mistakes; just agree in the most simple and direct way possible.

What responses could you make in answer to the criticisms cited above? Jot them down here, being as direct as possible and not putting yourself down in the process:

....

....

....

....

Our suggestions for the responses would be:

'Yes. I know I am untidy.'
'Yes. I'm sorry I'm late.'
'I'm sorry; I was miles away. I wasn't listening.'
'Yes. I'm sorry I've been irritable recently.'

It is important to say the words 'untidy' or 'late' or 'not listening' even though you may be reluctant to admit to your faults at first. By saying the words, you will reduce their importance from that of an unmentionable horror to a small, easily acceptable fact.

Invalid Criticism

This includes, of course, any criticism which is untrue or meant to put you down. Sometimes it is difficult to recognise whether criticism is valid or invalid, for instance someone may accuse you of being lazy. You may think you are hard-working, but then you remember the occasions when you have been lazy, so you accept the criticism, even though you feel hard done by. You have to ask yourself if this criticism is generally true of you – do you 'own' it? If not, you can assertively refuse to own an unfair generalisation:

'That's not generally true! I am very hard-working,' or:
'That's not true. It's unfair to take one instance, when I generally work very hard.'

Receiving Criticism

In the previous section, you drew up a short list of criticisms that people have made of you or that you are afraid people might make. Can you now expand this list and divide it into valid and invalid criticisms? Think of five of each – but make sure that you only put criticisms that you 'own' and accept as true in the valid list.

	Valid	Invalid
1	....	....
2	....	....
3	....	....
4	....	....
5	....	....

The next exercise will help you cope with the next time you are on the receiving end of criticism. You can do it alone, or with a friend. If you are with a friend, give the list to them so they can give you both valid and invalid criticisms. You can practise the techniques out loud of accepting and assertively rejecting the criticisms. Alternatively, imagine someone is making these criticisms of you: hear their exact words in your head; visualise the scene – where they are sitting or standing, how they look at you and so on – and then reply clearly and firmly.

Remember to use assertive body language and tone of voice, as well as using assertive wording. If it helps you to work it out in advance, you can use these spaces to write down the exact criticism and your replies:

Criticism: ....

Your reply: ....

....

Criticism: ....

Your reply: ....

....

Criticism: ....

Your reply: ....

....

Criticism: ....

Your reply: ....

....

Remember that valid criticism applies to only one aspect of your behaviour, and not to the whole person. Let us just restore the balance by looking at *positive* aspects of your behaviour. Use this space to write down five positive things about yourself:

1 ....

2 ....

3 ....

4 ....

5 ....

Giving or receiving invalid criticism (especially put-downs) lowers our self-esteem, unless we find effective techniques of rejecting it. Read your list of five good things again. And again. You don't need to put other people down, nor do you need to let other people do it to you.

So, how do you give criticism in a way that is constructive and not hurtful?

Giving Criticism

Hopefully, reminding yourself of your good points should have taken the sting out of your criticisms of yourself. The same applies to times when you have to criticise other people. Saying something positive about the person first is one way we can make our criticism easier for them to accept, and more constructive.

'I'm very pleased with your work and your attitude, but you can't wear your jeans at work.'

● Be even handed. Give praise where you can. This helps the recipient remember that their good points are valued by you, so your criticism can be accepted without loss of self-esteem.

● Make sure your criticism refers to specific behaviour and does not label the whole person. For example, compare:

'You're such an untidy person, your room is always a mess,' with
'You haven't tidied your room. Could you do it now?'

● Make a clear, constructive suggestion as to what you'd like them to do. Vague hints about what you would like are no help to the other person, so make your request specific, such as:

'Thank you for the report you have just finished. It was excellent. However, your desk is in a terrible mess. Can you take some time to tidy it up?'

● Express your feelings honestly. Do not assume that they are aware of the effect their behaviour is having on you. Avoid angry scenes, choose your time and place, and state your feelings calmly and without hostility. For example:

'When you interrupt me like that it makes me feel as though what I am saying is not important. Please try not to.'

Think of a criticism you have made, or would like to make, of someone else. Is it a valid criticism? How can you apply the techniques described above to ensure your criticism is made in a way that is not aggressive, but constructive and friendly and easier for them to accept? Write one or two suggestions below:

....

....

....

....

A few more words on giving and receiving criticism.

There are some subjects that we feel strongly about, and we cannot help reacting badly if someone criticises us on those points. Often it is something very personal that others are unaware we feel sensitive about, such as the size of our nose, our weight or height, our accent or education, our race or colour or beliefs. We all have them – our sensitive spots. The only way to make this sort of personal criticism more bearable is by the method you practised above; by accepting the criticism and saying the actual words to 'take the heat' out of your feelings. When you become less sensitive, you will start to feel more positive about these things.

If someone else has remarked on one of these sensitive spots, the chances are that it is accidental, that they have no idea of the effect it will have on you, and this is when you need to state your feelings. Or they may be aware of your sensitivity and are attempting a put-down. In any case, you should be able to deal better with those situations now, having done the work in this book.

Finally, remember the value of praise in restoring someone's self-esteem. Particularly after a long or difficult discussion, when perhaps there has been criticism on both sides, how valuable and important it can be to remind yourselves of the other's good points: it restores confidence in the relationship. So try to end on a positive note, such as: 'I'm glad we've had this chance to talk things through. I always value your opinions.'

Giving and Receiving Compliments

To some extent we have already touched on this subject and you should already have an appreciation of the importance of giving compliments or 'positive feedback' in enhancing people's sense of self-worth. So why don't we accept compliments more readily, when we know how good they make us feel? Jot down your thoughts on this in the space below:

....

....

....

....

Perhaps you have given reasons such as: 'because we were told as children not to be vain or boastful about our talents', or 'because it is embarrassing'. When someone says you are clever you feel as if they've found out that you secretly aspire to cleverness. Or maybe you feel that people only pay you a compliment when they want something; their compliment is false.

These are all defensive reactions – we don't want to believe what they say. It is true that people sometimes give compliments to try to manipulate you. As with criticism, the main art here is to distinguish between the genuine and the false compliment. You can do this in the same way as you did with valid and invalid criticism: ask yourself, 'is it true? Am I able to accept and own this praise?' If you know perfectly well that the compliment refers to something you are proud of and like about yourself, or something you have been trying very hard at, then accept it! You deserve it!

Accepting compliments

False modesty not only belittles your abilities, it makes a fool of the person doing the complimenting, and it can be very annoying. So avoid a brush-off such as 'it was nothing' or 'I'm not very good at it really'. Accept the compliment gracefully – or better still, assertively. Try this:

'Thank you for the compliment. I have been working really hard at loosing weight. I'm glad you noticed it.'
'I'm glad you liked the meal. I like trying new recipes.'
'Yes. I wanted to produce a good report. It's nice to know I succeeded.'

Look now at your list of five positive things about yourself. Is there anything you want to add? If you can, do this exercise with a friend. Exchange lists and practise giving and receiving compliments. If you are doing it alone, visualise who will make the compliment and what they will say, how and where. Practise aloud, visualising how you will sit or stand, and how you will look as you say the exact words you will use to accept the compliment assertively. If you would like to plan what you will say, use this space:

....

....

....

As with giving and receiving criticism, using the specific words takes some of the heat, or embarrassment, out of the situation. If you can also follow up by showing your feelings of pleasure at receiving such a compliment, so much the better – it lets the other person know their remarks are valued. What kind of facial expression might you use? We hope you answered: a smile.

Giving compliments

We often take people for granted, especially those we care about most. We assume that they must know how we feel, that they are clever and that we admire their abilities. But the previous work we have done shows you cannot expect people to know these things unless you can tell them; and the more simple, clear and direct you can be the better. So the first golden rule is:

- Express your feelings positively and assertively.

By now you know that 'assertively' does not mean going over the top! Gushing 'I think you are wonderful' is vague, too unspecific to be helpful and reeks of flattery.

- Keep it simple.

- Be specific about what it is you are complimenting.

- Be clear and confident of your right to express your opinions.

- Be honest.

Now think of five compliments that you would like to give but have always felt too shy or embarrassed to say. Remember the good effect that accepting compliments naturally and easily had on you, and the good effect it has on our relationships. Even bosses like to receive recognition of a good job well done!

Following On

What would you like to achieve in the next year? Look again at your Daydream Believer and use it to help you. Do you want to build your own boat in your spare time? Have a child and become a full-time home-maker? Be sitting in the director's chair a year from now?

Write five goals here:

1 ....

....

2 ....

....

3 ....

....

4 ....

....

5 ....

....

How can you work assertively towards achieving them?

1 ....

....

2 ....

....

3 ....

....

4 ....

....

5 ....

....

Keep this book handy and re-read sections; revisit the activities and your thoughts and feelings for as long as you need to. A positive process has been underway since you opened the book, and we wish you luck.

Lifeskills

Personal Development Series

Other titles available in this series are:

TIME MANAGEMENT:
Conquer the Clock

Time Management is about recognising that time is limited, setting clear priorities and objectives for yourself, and then ensuring that you achieve them. *Conquer the Clock* will:

- show you how to analyse your present use of time, including the concept of sold, maintenance and discretionary time

- help you identify the priorities in your life and rank them in order of importance

- introduce you to the many different ways and styles of managing time.

COMMUNICATION:
Time to Talk

'It is tempting to assume that our communication skills come to us as part of our natural development. Yet some people develop into very effective communicators, while others barely reach survival level.' Without communication there would be no relationships between people; sharing ideas, giving opinions, finding out what we need to know, working out differences, giving positive criticism and expressing our feelings are examples of the kind of face-to-face communication which is essential to our everyday life and work with other people. *Time to Talk* will:

- explain how to recognise and prevent 'communication breakdown' at work and at home
- help you to identify helpful and unhelpful ways of communicating
- encourage you to develop and improve your interpersonal communication skills.

TRANSITIONS:
The Challenge of Change

'When a chrysalis metamorphoses into a butterfly it is a natural process, it is something that must happen for the insect to become beautiful, to fly, to mate, to realise its potential.' This is a good symbol to use about facing our own transitions, because we need to change to realise our potential. Change is essential and creates opportunities, but it often causes stress and worry. Modern life is full of changes; the list is endless. *The Challenge of Change* will:

- help you to identify the different types of transition and their patterns
- help you make sense of the confusing feelings you may experience after an upheaval
- emphasise the benefits that can come from transitions, and provide a step-by-step, comprehensive guide to managing change positively.

Other Mercury titles from Lifeskills are:

BUILD YOUR OWN RAINBOW
Barrie Hopson and Mike Scally

A Lifeskills Workbook for Career and Life Management

Adopted by the Open University for Work Choices, a Community Education course.

Build Your Own Rainbow is the first of a new series of Lifeskills guides. It contains 40 exercises that will help answer the questions:

- who am I?
- where am I now?
- how satisfied am I?
- what changes do I want?
- how do I make them happen?
- what if it doesn't work out?

In the process of doing this, readers will discover what is important to them about work, where their main interests lie, what their transferable skills are and which career pattern would best suit them. They will be helped to set personal and career objectives, to make action plans and to take greater charge of their lives.

12 STEPS TO SUCCESS THROUGH SERVICE
Barrie Hopson and Mike Scally

A Lifeskills Management Guide

Satisfying the customer is the single most vital factor in business success and the main priority in any business must be to win and keep the customer. This book provides a complete programme to achieve success through service in twelve crucial steps:

- decide on your core business
- know your customer
- create your wisdom
- define your moments of truth
- give good service to one another
- manage the customer's experience
- profit from complaints
- stay close to your customer
- design and market the service programme
- set service criteria
- reward service excellence
- develop the service programme.

Lifeskills is one of the leading providers of Quality Service Programmes in the English-speaking world.

POSITIVE LEADERSHIP
Mike Pegg

How to Build a Winning Team
A Lifeskills Management Guide

Good leaders have many features in common. They develop a clear vision, they inspire their people, gain commitment from them, then guide their teams to success. This sounds easy in theory, but how is it done?

This is a book written for top teams, managers, and anybody who is a leader of people. It offers a framework for leadership and teamwork, with concrete ideas which can be incorporated into the daily work plan.

It focuses on how to:

- provide positive leadership
- be a positive team member
- build a positive culture
- set a positive goal, and get commitment to reaching it
- be a positive implementer
- build a positive reputation
- get positive results
- continue to build a positive and successful team.